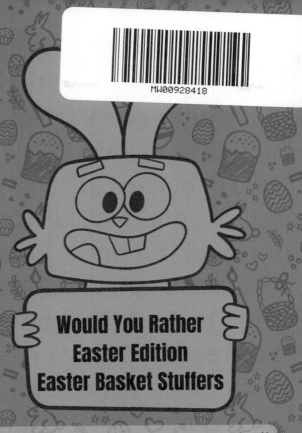

**Would You Rather**
**Easter Edition**
**Easter Basket Stuffers**

Published by Daniel G. Campbell
Copyright © 2022 Daniel G. Campbell

ISBN: 9798385773794
Printed in the USA

# Welcome to Easter
## Would You Rather

Hippity-hoppity how do you feel about choices!? Are you quick on your feet like a bunny or would you rather waddle like a duckie? "Would you rather" is all about choices! So if you read "Would you rather be a human-sized bunny or bunny-sized human?" It is up to you to hop into action and think up an awesome answer!

Have fun and answer honestly, but remember you have to choose even if the options aren't your favorite. You can explain your reasoning or stand by your choices silently like the noble Easter Bunny! No matter how you play, this game will reveal so much about anyone playing and is sure to bring about hours of laughter and fun!

Have a hopping good time playing this classic game and happy Easter!

# Would you rather ...

## Table of content:

## Easter Chickens

# <u>Would you rather ...</u>

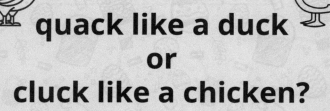

## quack like a duck
## or
## cluck like a chicken?

........................................................................

## be a fancy-feathered chicken
## or
## a smooth-feathered chicken?

........................................................................

## sit on a nest of eggs
## or
## lead the baby chicks?

<u>Easter Chickens</u>

have chicken claws
or
a chicken beak?

.................................................

be the rooster in charge
of waking everyone up
or
the hen in charge of the
eggs?

.................................................

be a hatched chick
or
a chick in the egg for one
day?

have a rooster comb
or
a rooster wattle?

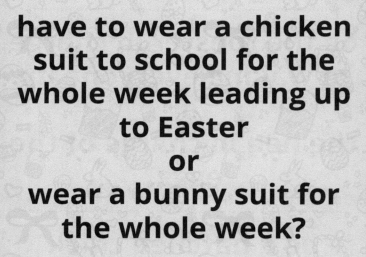

have to wear a chicken
suit to school for the
whole week leading up
to Easter
or
wear a bunny suit for
the whole week?

roost like a hen
or
nest like a duck?

be the top chicken in the pecking order
**or**
somewhere in the middle?

.................................................................

get a rubber chicken in your Easter basket
**or**
a whoopie cushion?

.................................................................

have to wave your arms like chicken wings every time you found an egg
**or**
hop up and down like a rabbit at every egg?

# <u>Would you rather ...</u>

find a chicken egg with a live chick inside an egg among your Easter eggs or a baby bunny in your basket?

.................................................

pet a downy chick
or
snuggle a full-grown hen?

.................................................

have to do a chicken hop-fly up and down all stairs for Easter week
or
wiggle your bunny nose every time someone said your name?

## <u>Easter Chickens</u>

## <u>Easter Rabbits</u>

## live in a rabbit hutch
## or
## a bunny burrow?

................................................................

## work with the Easter Bunny
## or
## the Tooth Fairy?

................................................................

## be able to wiggle your nose
## or
## twist your ears like a bunny?

## <u>Easter Rabbits</u>

**have a fluffy bunny tail
or
long rabbit ears?**

·····················································

**sit perfectly still like a
bunny
or
hop high like a rabbit?**

·····················································

**be a baby bunny (a kit)
or
a baby duck (a duckling)?**

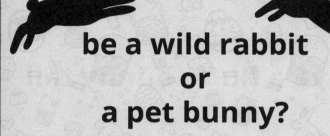

**be a wild rabbit
or
a pet bunny?**

....................................................

**have to be silent like
a rabbit
or
chirp your words like
a bird?**

....................................................

**for one day only eat
veggies like a bunny
or
have to hop all day?**

## <u>Easter Rabbits</u>

# Would you rather ...

**be able to burrow like a bunny**
**or**
**fly like a duck?**

...................................................

**have to carry the basket**
**or**
**hide the eggs?**

...................................................

**do the bunny hop**
**or**
**the chicken dance?**

## Easter Rabbits

be as fast as a rabbit
or
able to jump as high?

.....................................................

be a bionic Easter bunny
that could jump super
high
or
be a super spring duck
that could quack crazy
loud?

.....................................................

have the legs of a bunny
and the ears of a duck
or
the legs of a duck and
the ears of a bunny?

take a photo with the
Easter bunny
or
Santa Claus?

---

hop down the bunny
trail
or
waddle to the duck
pond?

---

have a spring chicken
or
a spring duck fill-in for
the Easter bunny?

wear the Easter Bunny's
pastel vest to school
or
a pair of bunny ears?

---

have big bunny teeth for
a day
or
strong bunny legs for a
day?

---

## Easter Eggs

# Would you rather ...

## make a striped egg
## or
## a solid-colored egg?

-------------------------------------

## get a plastic egg
## or
## a candy egg?

-------------------------------------

## eat 10 chocolate eggs
## or
## 10 hard-boiled eggs?

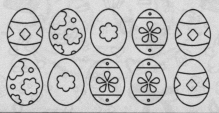

## Easter Eggs

## hide eggs
## or
## find eggs?

......................................................

## be on an egg hunt
## or
## coloring eggs?

......................................................

## find plastic eggs
## or
## hard-boiled eggs?

## Easter Eggs

# Would you rather ...

**eat deviled eggs
or
scrambled eggs?**

**use egg decorating
stickers
or
markers?**

**eat Easter brunch
or
go on an egg hunt?**

## Easter Eggs

color eggs with
springtime pastels
or
bright neon colors?

---

find a nest of eggs
or
see baby ducklings
walking to the pond?

---

build your nest low and
covered like a duck
or
high and hidden like a
robin?

**Easter Eggs**

hatch from a brown
chicken egg
or
a blue robin's egg?

..............................................

discover that all the
Easter eggs were
accidentally swapped
with snake eggs
or
ostrich eggs?

..............................................

shrink to the size of a
chick before the egg hunt
or
grow to the size
of a spring bear?

<u>Easter Eggs</u>

## Easter Ducks

## Easter Ducks

**have to quack all day
or
waddle like a duck all day?**

......................................................

**be the first duckling in the line
or
the last duckling in the line?**

......................................................

**have a duck bill
or
feathers?**

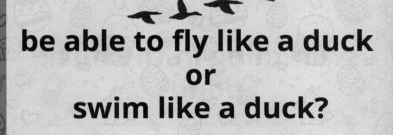

## be able to fly like a duck
## or
## swim like a duck?

........................................................

## be able to dive like a duck
## or
## paddle for hours like a duck?

........................................................

## have a duck bill
## or
## webbed feet?

# Would you rather ...

be in the duck nest
or
swimming in the duck pond?

........................................................

follow a group of ducks
or
lead a group of ducks?

........................................................

be a duck that dives for food
or
a duck that eats the bread from people in the park?

## Easter Ducks

# Would you rather ...

have colorful feathers like a mallard duck
or
white feathers like a Pekin duck?

have to quack every time you dipped an egg in dye
or
shake your tail feathers every time you ate a jelly bean?

be a human-sized duckling
or
a human-sized chick?

**Easter Ducks**

# Would you rather ...

redecorate your sibling's room to look like a duck's nest
or
rabbit's burrow?

.......................................................................

shake your tail feathers
or
waddle around?

.......................................................................

have webbed feet but not be able to swim
or
have long rabbit feet but not be able to jump?

## Easter Ducks

## Easter Baskets

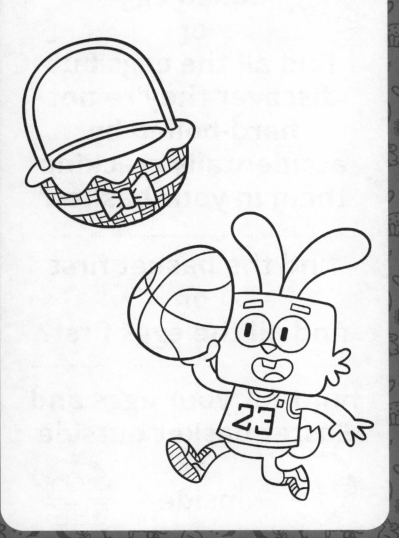

never find one hard-
boiled egg
or
find all the eggs but
discover they're not
hard-boiled by
accidentally cracking
them in your basket?

....................................................

find the basket first
or
find all the eggs first?

....................................................

hunt for your eggs and
Easter basket outside
or
inside?

## Easter Baskets

find an Easter basket
filled with toys and gear
for outside
or
crafts and art supplies?

........................................................

find a basket the size of
the Easter Bunny
or
the size of a wild bunny?

........................................................

have to carry your whole
neighborhood's Easter
baskets for one hour
or
juggle five Easter eggs
for 10 minutes?

## Easter Baskets

**find an Easter basket
full of candy
or
full of toys?**

---

**find an Easter basket
with tons of candy but
you have to face an
angry chicken to get it
or
a hyper-hopping rabbit?**

## Easter Baskets

# Would you rather ...

have to sing the chicken dance to get your Easter basket
or
sing the bunny hop?

.................................................................

fill your bedroom three feet deep with that funny Easter basket grass
or
three feet deep with jelly beans?

## Easter Baskets

## all eggs be the size of a basketball
## or
## all eggs be bouncing balls?

## <u>Easter Candy</u>

<u>Easter Candy</u>

# Would you rather ...

get a solid chocolate
bunny
or
a hollow chocolate
bunny?

................................................

have a fruit-filled
chocolate egg
or
a cream-filled chocolate
egg?

................................................

eat jelly beans
or
chocolate eggs?

## Easter Candy

## eat marshmallow chicks
## or
## almond eggs?

....................................................

## find chocolate candy in
## your Easter basket
## or
## fruity candy?

....................................................

## know the flavor of the
## jelly bean before eating it
## or
## take your chances?

## be a chocolate bunny
### or
## a marshmallow chick?

......................................................

## have malted milk ball eggs
### or
## chewing gum eggs?

......................................................

## eat Easter candy
### or
## carrot cake?

# Would you rather ...

eat rice cereal treat egg
or
chocolate crunch eggs?

---

have a sour candy
or
a sweet candy?

---

have candied fruit
or
marshmallow candy?

## Easter Candy

find a candy surprise in
your egg
or
a toy?

---

have the rice cereal eggs
from the store
or
homemade rice cereal
eggs?

---

have a cream egg
or
a marshmallow egg?

## Easter Candy

# Would you rather ...

get an egg with a jelly center
or
a bubblegum center?

..............................................................

eat 100 jelly beans
or
eat 100 chocolate malted eggs?

..............................................................

find a chocolate bunny that really hops
or
a marshmallow chick that really chirps?

**Easter Candy**

face an army of
chocolate bunnies
or
an army of
marshmallow chicks?

get a bag of popcorn-
flavored jelly beans
or
Easter-colored candy
corn?

## <u>Easter Food</u>

## eat a bunny cake
## or
## hot cross buns?

...........................................................

## eat an Easter ham
## or
## Easter lamb?

...........................................................

## eat a spring lemon cookie
## or
## a spring bird's nest cookie?

## have candied carrots
## or
## raw carrots and dip?

---

## have Easter dinner
## or
## Easter brunch?

---

## eat a carrot cake
## or
## a rhubarb pie?

**have spring asparagus**
**or**
**string beans?**

...................................................................

**have a banana cream pie**
**or**
**a coconut cream pie?**

...................................................................

**have an Easter dinner**
**or**
**an Easter dessert?**

## eat Easter food
## or
## help make Easter food?

...................................................

## have a lemon tart
## or
## a key lime pie for Easter
## dessert?

...................................................

## eat spring greens like
## arugula
## or
## spring carrots?

cook the springtime
feast
or
eat it?

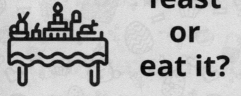 

........................................

have a bunny-shaped
cake pop
or
a chick-shaped cake
pop?

........................................

have mashed potatoes
or
scalloped potatoes with
Easter dinner?

## Springtime

**have a bouquet of
tulips
or
a bouquet of lilies?**

........................................................

**smell the spring flowers
or
look at them?**

........................................................

**listen to the birds sing
or
walk through the
flowers?**

# Would you rather ...

## see a robin's egg hatch
## or
## tadpoles swimming?

........................................................

## smell lilacs
## or
## spring lilies?

........................................................

## visit a spring pond
## or
## a spring meadow?

## Springtime

# Would you rather ...

experience spring in the country
or
in the city?

........................................................

have a spring picnic
or
take a spring hike?

........................................................

do one hour of spring cleaning
or
one hour of homework?

## Springtime

be a baby animal in the springtime
or
its parent?

---

see the cherry blossoms
or
look for four-leaf clovers?

---

make flower chains with dandelions
or
listen to spring rain?

get caught in a spring
shower
or
jump in the puddles
after the rain?

.....................................................

take a spring bike ride
or
play catch outside?

.....................................................

tip-toe through spring
tulips
or
leap through the lilies?

**plant a spring garden
or
make some springtime
donations?**

...........................................

**wear shorts for the first
time of the year
or
short sleeves?**

...........................................

**watch the bees work
or
blow bubbles in the
spring sun?**

## Springtime

# <u>Would you rather ...</u>

smell green spring grass
or
the spring air after the rain?

........................................................

be on a spring beach
or
a spring forest?

........................................................

visit a farm in the spring
or
take a walk in the prairie?

<u>Springtime</u>

# Would you rather ...

see the worms after rain
or
see the rolly-pollies come out from under stones?

................................................................

your Easter best every day for a year
or
have a dressed-down Easter?

................................................................

see the spring flowers
or
the first green grass?

## Springtime

# <u>Would you rather ...</u>

visit a spring farmer's market
or
plant the veggies yourself?

......................................................

 **be a rabbit**
or
a carrot farmer?

......................................................

have to wear only Easter colors forever
or
only be able to eat Easter ham as your protein forever?

<u>Springtime</u>

only be able to listen to "Peter Cottontail" from now on
or
only be able to dance the bunny hop?

..................................................

wear spring pastels
or
fun springtime floral prints?

..................................................

see a spring fawn during a hike
or
find a nest of eggs during a hike?

paint hearts on every
egg you see
or
every bunny you see fall
in love with you?

---

travel with a rabbit
around the world
or
play egg hunting with
the Easter bunny?

Easter Bunny

# Would you rather ...

# General Questions

have dragon wings or the ability to breathe fire?

---

be able to control the rain or able to control the outside temperature?

---

see a movie at the theater or the drive in?

---

wear a halloween costume to school or wear a purple wig for a week?

**have a pet lion
or a pet wolf?**

····················································

**have a longer winter
break
or a longer summer
break?**

····················································

**have dessert for
breakfast everyday
or breakfast for dinner
everyday?**

····················································

**go to the moon
or go to the top of a
mountain?**

be a butterfly
or a honey bee?

---

have ten free toys
or ten free books?

---

listen to the same song
for a month straight
or listen to a new song
everyday?

---

sing in front of a crowd
or perform in a play?

have the ability to turn invisible
or have the ability to pause time?

........................................................

be able to swing like a monkey
or run like a cheetah?

........................................................

be stuck on an island with one book
or one video game?

........................................................

be able to breathe underwater
or breathe in outer space?

be able to understand fish
or be able to understand dogs?

..................................................

live in a treehouse
or a house with a glass ceiling?

..................................................

have the ability to time travel
or the ability to teleport?

..................................................

have an unlimited amount of art supplies
or an unlimited amount of coloring books?

be able to play any instrument
or be able to speak any language?

........................................................

be able to swim fast
or run fast?

........................................................

have super strength or the ability to move things with your mind?
live in the future or in the past?

........................................................

have a pet shark
or a pet octopus?

see a Pegasus
or a mermaid?

---

live in the mountains
or on a beach?

---

have vampire teeth
or elf ears?

---

watch the same movie
for a month straight
or watch a new movie
every day for a month
straight?

be able to control rocks or water?

..................................................

pick on beverage to drink for a year
or one food to eat for a year?

..................................................

live in an RV
or on a cruise boat?

..................................................

have a flying car
or a submarine?

**meet an alien
or a dinosaur?**

......................................................

**have a talking cat
or a robot?**

......................................................

**be able to read animals'
minds
or know the definition
to every word?**

......................................................

**switch bodies with a
plant
or an animal?**

be able to sit on a cloud or hold a rainbow?

..................................................

have superpowers or the ability to do magic?

..................................................

be able to walk on walls and ceilings or fly?

..................................................

have an unlimited supply of snacks or an unlimited supply of video games?

have a beak for a nose
or a nose like a cat?

..................................................

have dog ears
or a tail?

..................................................

always have
mismatched shoes
or always have
mismatched socks?

..................................................

have to fight 100
mouse sized elephants
or one elephant sized
mouse?

travel the world
or travel the solar
system?

...............................................................

have the chance to
write a book
or the chance to create
a new game?

...............................................................

not be able to drink
soda
or not be able to eat
chips?

...............................................................

learn to play guitar
or learn dance?

get ten small presents
or one big present?

................................................................

have fangs like a
vampire
or pegasus wings?

................................................................

be able to draw
anything
or be able to make
any dessert?

................................................................

have a bike that
could fly
or a skateboard that
could skate on water?

fly a plane
or drive a motorcycle?

....................................................

get to meet a fictional
character
or a celebrity?

....................................................

be immune to getting a
cold
or unable to break any
bones?

....................................................

be a doctor
or a lawyer?

**take a train
or a ship to travel?**

......................................................

**eat a whole lemon
or a large spoon of hot
sauce?**

......................................................

**be a medieval knight
or a ninja?**

......................................................

**never be able to wear
socks
or never be able to wear
shoes?**

have a pen that could be any color
or headphones that could play any song?

---

be as big as a blue whale
or as small as a tree frog?

---

be able to read very fast
or write very fast?

---

have exceptional hearing
or exceptional sight?

have the world's softest blanket
or the world's comfiest bed?

---

have pink hair
or purple eyes?

---

have a glowing crystal as a lamp
or a glowing jellyfish?

---

be able to travel to another galaxy
or travel to the deepest part of the ocean?

get to pick all of your birthday gifts until you're 18
or pick one big gift to receive at 18?

...................................................................

have to only eat frozen food
or only eat boxed food?

...................................................................

meet an elf
or a fairy?

...................................................................

never be able to play any sports
or never be able to play any instruments?

design a new video
game
or direct a movie?

.....................................................

live on the beach
or in the woods?

.....................................................

have a big mohawk
or hair down to your
ankles?

.....................................................

ride on the back of an
orca whale
or ride on the back of a
giraffe?

**never be able to eat ice cream again
or never be able to eat cake again?**

........................................................

**learn karate
or how to shoot a bow and arrow?**

........................................................

**have a phoenix
or a griffin for a pet?**

........................................................

**have a book with a story that never ended
or a coloring book that never ran out of new pages?**

have an eraser that
could erase anything
or a pencil that brought
your drawings to life?

......................................................

have a pillow that never
loses its fluff
or a stuffed animal that
stayed new forever?

......................................................

be a pilot
or an actor?

......................................................

have the ability to paint
anything you wanted
or the ability to cook
anything you wanted?

travel to all fifty states
or travel to five
different countries?

..............................................

have eight arms like an
octopus
or stinging tentacles like
a jellyfish?

..............................................

be able to control your
dreams
or control when you fall
asleep and wake up?

..............................................

have butterfly wings
or bird wings?

vacation on the beach
or in a forest?

......................................

be able to camouflage
yourself like a
chameleon
or able to shoot needles
like a porcupine?

......................................

never have to study
again
or never have to do
chores again?

......................................

eat plain toast
or plain noodles?

win every board game
or never lose rock paper
scissors?

...............................................................

spend a day inside of a
cartoon
or a book?

...............................................................

have an indoor pool
or an indoor bowling
alley?

...............................................................

live in a castle
or on another planet?

be able to transform your room into whatever you want to or able to make the clothes you  want magically appear in your closet?

..................................................

be really good at inventing things
or really good at making music?

..................................................

live in the city
or the countryside?

wear your clothes inside out
or backward?

........................................................

play in the rain
or in the snow?

........................................................

go to the movies
or watch a movie at home?

........................................................

have the ability to fly
or be able to breath under
water?

........................................................

have to stay up all night
or sleep all read?

be without the Internet for a week or without your phone?

················································································

sail the world or fly around the world?

················································································

live on a farm
or live in a big city?

················································································

go without television or junk food for the rest of your life?

················································································

have a magic wand
or a magic carpet?

see a dinosaur or a dragon?

.........................................................

wear your pants backward or wear your shoes on the wrong feet?

.........................................................

visit a lost city or a Museum?

.........................................................

meet a mermaid or an elf?

.........................................................

have a camera as your eyes or a sound recorder as your ears?

live on the Moon
or live on Mars?

spoil a movie for friends that they haven't seen or have a friend spoil a movie that you haven't seen?

.................................................................

swim in a pool full of jelly or full of Nutella?

.................................................................

learn to pilot a plane
or learn to drive a race car?

.................................................................

own a pirate ship
or a private jet?

.................................................................

be able to control time
or control the weather?

be a teacher or a student?

..............................................

live without music
or without television?

..............................................

live in a tree house
or in a cave?

..............................................

be floating in a lifeboat on the
ocean or alone in a desert?

..............................................

never eat chocolate again or
never kiss anyone again?

..............................................

adopt cats or dogs?

be a doctor for people
or a vet?

..............................................

have a kangaroo
or koala as your pet?

..............................................

have a car that could fly
or a car that you could drive
underwater?

..............................................

possess the ability to smell
sounds
or be able to hear smells?

..............................................

be a monkey
or a bunny?

be a friend of a magical creature or an alien?

..................................................................

only eat your favorite food for the rest of your life or never eat it again?

..................................................................

have a water fight or a food fight?

..................................................................

eat worms or beetles if you had to survive?

..................................................................

be super strong or super fast?

..................................................................

take tea or coffee?

General questions

live in a house made of doughnuts or sleep in a bed made of jelly beans?

..................................................................

spend all night in a bookstore or in a supermarket?

..................................................................

have your uncle's hair or your grandfather's mustache?

..................................................................

trade toothbrushes with a stranger or exchange underwear?

..................................................................

live in a pond with some frogs, or live in a tree with some squirrels?

## General questions

ride a horse or drive a car?

.................................................

cook dinner
or clean up afterward?

.................................................

live without shampoo
or without toothpaste?

.................................................

have a small party
every month
or one big party every year?

.................................................

hold a cockroach or a worm?

.................................................

be loved by every
human you see or be
loved by every dog you see?

watch any movie you like in slow motion, or only watch movies other people choose but at regular speed?

........................................

travel to the past to see living dinosaurs or travel to past to see how the pyramids were built?

........................................

your drawings come to life or your songs become reality?

........................................

never have milk to have with your cereals or never have butter to put on your bread?

have stripes like a tiger
or rosettes like a jaguar?

...................................................................

have a gum stick in your hair
or step on it?

...................................................................

to be a shark in the sea
or a piranha in the Amazon?

...................................................................

spend the night alone at a
museum or camp outdoors?

...................................................................

be all alone in a desert
or in a jungle?

...................................................................

be able to see everything
or control anything?

never wear shoes
or never wear underwear?

................................................

go on a two-week vacation
anywhere you want,
or get a two-month vacation
at home?

................................................

have a cat-sized elephant
or an elephant-sized cat as a
pet?

................................................

be in your favorite video
game or be in your favorite
cartoon?

Made in United States
Troutdale, OR
03/20/2024